Structural Wonders

Parthenon

James De Medeiros

Weigl Publishers Inc.

Published by Weigl Publishers Inc.
350 5th Avenue, Suite 3304, PMB 6G
New York, NY 10118-0069

Website: www.weigl.com

Library of Congress Cataloging-in-Publication Data

De Medeiros, James.
  Parthenon / James De Medeiros.
     p. cm. -- (Structural wonders)
  Includes index.
  ISBN 978-1-59036-727-8 (hard cover : alk. paper) -- ISBN 978-1-59036-728-5 (soft cover :
alk. paper)
  1. Parthenon (Athens, Greece)--Juvenile literature. 2. Athens (Greece)--Buildings, structures,
etc.--Juvenile literature. I. Title.
  NA281.D46 2008
  726'.120809385--dc22

                    2007012125

Printed in the United States of America
1 2 3 4 5 6 7 8 9 0 11 10 09 08 07

Photograph Credits
Every reasonable effort has been made to trace ownership and to obtain
permission to reprint copyright material. The publishers would be pleased
to have any errors or omissions brought to their attention so that they may
be corrected in subsequent printings.

All of the internet URLs given in the book were valid at the time of publication.
However, due to the dynamic nature of the Internet, some addresses may have
changed, or sites may have ceased to exist since publication. While the author
and publisher regret any inconvenience this may cause readers, no responsibility
for any such changes can be accepted by either the author or the publisher.

Project Coordinators: Heather C. Hudak, Heather Kissock
Design: Terry Paulhus

Contents

What is the Parthenon?

Ever since humans first developed tools, they have been building. All **cultures** and countries build structures. These structures can include churches, schools, houses, shopping malls, stadiums, towers, and office buildings. Some of these buildings, such as malls, may have many different purposes. Other buildings, such as schools, may be built with one clear idea in mind. In every case, structures are built using scientific principles that allow for the production of creative plans.

The Parthenon, located in Athens, Greece, is one of the earliest examples of such buildings. The Parthenon is a rectangular building with tall, white columns. It sits on top of a rocky hill. The building served as the temple of the **Acropolis**. Inside the Parthenon, the Greeks stored **treasury** funds, gifts, and a statue of Athena, the goddess of wisdom and war.

The Parthenon was built at the instruction of Pericles, a powerful political leader in Athens, during the period of 447–432 BC. At this time, Athens was experiencing great prosperity, and the decision was made to build the Parthenon in honor of the goddess Athena. A previous attempt to build a temple in honor of the goddess had been burnt by the Persians, who attacked Greece in 480 BC.

Pericles chose Ictinus to be the primary **architect** responsible for building the Parthenon. Ictinus designed a four-sided building that had a six-column, horizontal porch on each end. There were vertical columns around all four sides.

While the Parthenon is no longer a place of worship or a treasury, it is difficult to imagine Greece without the spectacular structure.

Quick Bites

- The statue of Athena was almost 39 feet (12 meters) high. It was made of gold and ivory.
- The Parthenon contains two chambers. At one time, the Eastern chamber housed the statue of Athena. The Western chamber housed the treasury.

Building History

From 480 to 479 BC, the Persians invaded and burnt the temples on the Acropolis. In 447, Pericles decided that, since Athens was enjoying such great prosperity, the time had come to restore the Acropolis to its former state. Pericles' plan was to build the Parthenon on the exact same place as the previous temple that had been destroyed by the Persians. His idea was to make the Parthenon the most amazing shrine to the goddess Athena. He chose Ictinus as his main architect, and also brought in another architect, Kallikrates, to help. Phidias, a **sculptor**, was hired to design a statue of the goddess. When finished, the Parthenon was a beautiful structure made entirely with marble from Mount Pentelicus, which is about 10 miles (16 kilometers) away from Athens.

Phidias is considered to be one of the greatest sculptors of ancient Greece.

Many of Pericles' political enemies did not like the way the structure was built. They felt that too much of the public's funds were spent on the building. The total cost of the structure is not known. However, the Parthenon cost more to build than any other temple in Greece at that time. It took many years to pay for the project.

Restoration work is often done to the Parthenon and the Acropolis.

TIMELINE OF CONSTRUCTION

489-480 BC: Themistocles starts the construction of the first Parthenon.

480 BC: The Persians attack and destroy the older Parthenon. The Athenians eventually defeat the Persians.

479-449 BC: The decision is made to make Athens a strong city both politically and economically. Rebuilding the temple is not a priority.

449 BC: Pericles decides to rebuild the temple on the Acropolis.

447-432 BC: Pericles hires Ictinus, Kallikrates, and Phidias to work on the construction of the new Parthenon. It is completed in 432 BC.

AD 500-600: The Parthenon is turned into a Christian church.

1460: Under Turkish rule, the Parthenon becomes a mosque.

1687: An attack by the Venetians destroys the middle portion of the Parthenon.

1801: British ambassador Lord Elgin removes sculptures from the Parthenon.

The Acropolis was the center of activity in Athens.

The Parthenon remained a shrine to Athena until the sixth century, when the Greeks turned it into a **Christian** church. It remained a church for nearly 900 years. In the fifteenth century, the Turks invaded Greece and changed the building into a **mosque**. The Parthenon changed little over the next 200 years.

In 1687, the Venetians attacked the Parthenon and shot a cannonball at the center of the building. This destroyed the middle portion of the structure. More damage occurred under Turkish rule when parts of the Parthenon were torn down and used as building materials. In the eighteenth century, some of the sculptures inside the Parthenon were sold to tourists from western Europe.

Phidias supervised the production of what would later beome known as the Elgin Marbles.

In 1801, Lord Elgin, the British ambassador of Constantinople, present-day Istanbul, received permission from the Turkish Sultan to take sculptures from the building. These sculptures, called the Elgin Marbles, are on display at the British Museum in London, England. More than 200 years later, the Greek government continues to ask for the pieces to be returned to Greece.

The triangular areas at the top of the Parthenon are called the pediments. They feature statues based on Greek mythology.

Big Ideas

Ictinus' passion for mathematics is shown in all of his structures. His appreciation and understanding of mathematical relationships is the main reason that he used ratios in his structures. Ratios measure the size of two things in relation to each other. They show how many times one can be contained by the other.

When building the Parthenon, Ictinus used the 4:9 ratio to determine measurements of length, width, height, and **diameter**. Therefore, the length of the temple was slightly more than twice its width. Likewise, the distance between the columns was slightly more than the diameter of the columns. It was believed that using this ratio gave the structure a harmonious appearance. Ictinus used this ratio to make all of his buildings seem more beautiful than those built prior to the Parthenon.

When the Parthenon was built, its columns curved outward in the middle. Ictinus did this to overcome an **optical illusion**. From far away, a vertical straight line is seen as slightly slanted. The curves were planned so that the building would look straight when it was seen in the distance. These line adjustments are called Doric refinements. They made the building look as though it only had straight lines, when it really had none. The upper portions of the columns lean inward as well, helping to create the appearance of straight lines.

Web Link:
To find out more about Doric columns, go to www.cmhpf.org/kids/dictionary/ClassicalOrders.html

1) Ictinus used Doric columns in his design for the Parthenon. 2) The Monument in London is a Doric column that was built to commemorate the Great Fire of London in 1666. 3) The Lincoln Memorial has 38 Doric columns.

Profile:
Ictinus, Kallikrates, and Phidias

Many historians believe Ictinus was the primary architect for the Parthenon. He received help on the project from Kallikrates, who served as either a secondary architect or a **contractor**. Phidias, an accomplished sculptor, also was involved in the creation of the project. Most information about Phidias, Kallikrates, and Ictinus comes from the writings of Plutarch, a biography writer in ancient Greece.

The Athenians chose Ictinus to lead the Parthenon's design team because of his outstanding abilities as an architect. Ictinus worked on many temples in Greece, including the Temple of Apollo at Bassai in Arcadia, Peloponnese. Ictinus used many of the same concepts and ideas for the Temple of Apollo that he used when building the Parthenon. As with the Parthenon, the Temple of Apollo combines various design styles, including the Doric, **Ionic**, and **Corinthian** styles.

Ictinus is responsible for the incomplete Telesterion built at Eleusis, Greece, northwest of Athens. The Persians destroyed this version of the Telesterion, and another one was built when Athens began experiencing economic growth. Ictinus' Telesterion had a smaller number of interior supports than the finished version. These supports were strategically placed around the

THE WORK OF ICTINUS, KALLIKRATES, AND PHIDIAS

Temple of Hephaestus

The Temple of Hephaestus is the most complete example of Ictinus' work remaining today. The temple, which uses Doric refinements, was built around 449 BC.

Temple of Apollo

Located in Bassai, Greece, the Temple of Apollo is believed to have been started around 420 BC and completed around 410 BC. It was built for Apollo, the god of healing and the Sun. Today, the temple is a UNESCO World Heritage Site.

Phidias' Statue of Zeus no longer exists today.

central shrine. By planning the structure this way, Ictinus was trying to lengthen the building over a larger distance. In doing so, he created the first centrally designed room. This was an idea that he used during the construction of the back room of the Parthenon.

The secondary architect involved in creating the Parthenon was Kallikrates. Kallikrates was the architect for the Temple of Athena Nike, which was finished around 420 BC. It is located at the Acropolis in Greece. From the **stylobate** to the top of the structure, it is only 11 feet (3.4 meters) tall. The Temple of Athena Nike features four columns on each end of the structure.

Phidias supervised all of the artistic works created for the Parthenon. His works are known for their grandeur, patriotism, dignity, and proportion. Phidias' work in the Parthenon uses the Golden Ratio. This ratio is based on the idea that rectangles with a length to width ratio of about 1:1.6 are most pleasing to the eye. The basic rule is that the length is always 1.6 times greater than the width. In the Parthenon, the spaces between the columns all form golden rectangles.

Temple of Athena Nike

The Temple of Athena Nike was built as a place of worship to the goddess, Athena. It was the first temple at the Acropolis to be built in the Ionic style. The temple was built on top of the ruins of a sixth-century temple to Athena that had been destroyed by the Persians in 480 BC. The four-column temple was built in stages, as funds were limited by war.

Statue of Zeus

Phidias carved the giant Statue of Zeus at Olympia around 435 BC. The statue stood 40 feet (12 m) tall and was one of the Seven Wonders of the Ancient World.

The Science Behind the Building

The materials used to build the Parthenon have lasted for a very long time. This is because of the properties, or qualities, these materials have. The choice to use these materials to build the Parthenon demonstrates Ictinus' understanding of certain scientific properties at work.

The Properties of Marble

Pericles wanted the Parthenon to be built better than any other building in history. Unlike some of the buildings in the 800–600 BC period that were made of wood or mud-brick, marble was used on the project. It provided the most beautiful result. More than 20,000 tons (18,000 tonnes) of marble were taken from Mount Pentelicus, one of the few places in the world where it can be found in great quality and quantity.

Marble is a soft rock. This means that it can be cut and shaped easily. The measurement of hardness scale (MOHS) determines the hardness of a stone based on how easily it can be scratched by grit or hard objects. On this scale, marble is a 3 out of 10. A hard piece of plastic rates about 2. It could not scratch marble. However, quartz, which measures 7, will scratch marble.

Even though marble is a soft rock, the Parthenon continues to stand after more than 2,000 years.

Marble's softness allowed the rock on the Parthenon to be sculpted into beautiful artistic shapes by creating grooves and straight edges. Marble also chips easily. Today, the use of marble has been greatly reduced, as it is widely believed that it is not as versatile as other stones. This is because it does not stand up as well as other materials in poor conditions.

The Properties of Iron and Lead

Marble blocks needed to be held in place at the Parthenon. Iron pins were used. Iron is a silver-white **element** that is easy to handle with the most basic tools. The iron pins were coated with lead. Lead is a bluish-white chemical element that has a melting point higher than 608° Fahrenheit (320° Celsius). This meant the pins could withstand the warmest Greek summers. Lead is easy to find, and it is easy to work with, as it can be bent by either hammering or light pressure. The lead helped to prevent corrosion from occurring. Corrosion happens when metal deteriorates, or rusts.

Years later, when efforts were made to reconstruct the Parthenon, the pins used were not coated with lead. The new pins rusted as a result of reactions to the environment. This rust further cracked the original marble. Recent efforts to reconstruct the Parthenon have proven to be far more successful, as titanium is now being used in place of iron. Titanium is a corrosion-resistant material that is strong and light.

Web Link:
To find out more about about rust, go to http://science.howstuffworks.com/question445.htm.

Science and Technology

Building any kind of structure requires three basic elements—technology, physical labor, and planning. During the era of the Parthenon, technology was not as advanced as it is today. The Greeks relied mainly on physical labor for construction.

Cutting the marble

Marble was heavy and expensive. Much of the sculpting was completed before moving the pieces to the Parthenon's site. The workers could not rely on electric power tools at the time, so they used simple tools and their physical strength to do the sculpting. The tools they used included picks, chisels, and drills. The workers placed the pick, chisel, or drill against the marble and tapped it with a hammer to cut pieces away. They then cut the marble to the appropriate height and width. This process continued until they had shaped the marble.

Transporting the marble

Most of the marble was transported to the Acropolis using large, four-wheeled wagons that were pulled by oxen. Wagons use a wheel and axle to move objects across distances. The wheel turns the axle. More than one wheel and axle pair can be used to move heavy objects. Mount Pentelicus is 10 miles (16 km) away from the Acropolis. Using these wagons, the trip from Mount Pentelicus to the Acropolis could take up to two days.

A chisel is a wedge-shaped, simple machine. A wedge is used to push things apart by converting motion on one end into a splitting motion at the other end. The splitting occurs at right angles to the blade.

A hook can be added to a pulley system to raise and lower objects.

Lifting devices

Once the marble arrived at the Acropolis, it had to be lifted from the wagons and put into place on the structure. To prepare the marble for lifting, one of two steps was taken. Workers would hollow out a section of the marble into a "U" shape, or they would make wedges near the ends of the slab. Different types of devices, including rope loops and tongs, were used to grab the marble. The workers would put the rope through the hollowed "U" section of the marble and use it to move the piece. Tongs were used to lift the other pieces. The tongs were inserted into the wedges so that the marble could be firmly grasped.

Workers used pulleys and cranes to move the marble piece. Pulleys are wheels that have grooves through which rope is strung. The number of wheels on a pulley system affect the amount of physical force needed to lift and move the marble. The more wheels the system had, the less force needed to move the marble.

The pulleys and rope were attached to hand-powered cranes. Once the marble was lifted from the ground, the workers could move it by swiveling the crane to where the marble had to be placed. The pulleys were used to lower the marble back to the ground.

Quick Bites

- More than 10,000 pieces of stone were used in the construction of the Parthenon.
- Workers did not always use wagons to transport the marble. Sometimes, they rolled the marble to the Acropolis.

Computer-Aided Design

Architects are trained professionals who work with clients to design structures. Before anything is built, they make detailed drawings or models. These plans are important tools that help people visualize what the structure will look like. A blueprint is a detailed diagram that shows where all the parts of the structure will be placed. Walls, doors, windows, plumbing, electrical wiring, and other details are mapped out on the blueprint. Blueprints act as a guide for engineers and builders during construction.

For centuries, architects and builders worked without the aid of computers. Sketches and blueprints were drawn by hand. Highly skilled drafters would draw very technical designs. Today, this process is done using computers and sophisticated software programs. Architects use CAD, or computer-aided design, throughout the design process. Early CAD systems used computers to draft building plans. Today's computer programs can do much more. They can build three-dimensional models and computer simulations of how a building will look. They can calculate the effects of different physical forces on the structure. Using CAD, today's architects can build more complex structures at lower cost and in less time.

Computer-aided design programs have been used since the 1960s.

Eye on Design

Computer-Aided Design and the making of *The Parthenon*

Computers are helping architects more every day. There are many different types of computer-aided design programs that are capable of presenting buildings in two or three-dimensions. Three-dimensional plans allow the architect to see a smaller scale version of the structure. In 2004, a math and computer engineer named Paul Debevec made a film about the use of computer graphics to create a three-dimensional representation of the Parthenon. Debevec and his team developed a special type of three-dimensional scanner to take images of the Parthenon and the Elgin Marbles. The scans were used to "reunite" the pieces of the Parthenon to show them as they may have looked in their original state. There are about 20 images showing the Parthenon and the Elgin Marbles as they are today and as they may have been hundreds of years ago.

The Elgin Marbles exhibit at the British Museum includes a video display that demonstrates how and where the sculptures were positioned on the Parthenon.

MEASURING THE PARTHENON

Location
The Parthenon is located at the Acropolis, in Athens, Greece.

Height
- The height of the Parthenon at completion in 432 BC was 65 feet (20 m).

Area
The Parthenon was built on the top step of a rectangular platform. The Parthenon is 228.1 feet (70 m) long and 101.4 feet (31 m) wide.

Weight
Modern estimates suggest that a single Parthenon column weighed between 63 and 119 tons (57 and 108 tonnes).

Other Interesting Facts
- More than four million people visit the Parthenon each year.
- Forty-six columns form the perimeter of the Parthenon.

Environmental Viewpoint

At the time the Parthenon was built, there was not much discussion about the environment. People did not worry about the effects the Parthenon's construction had on the surrounding area. They simply took what they needed and built where they wanted to build.

Unlike today, the construction methods used at that time had minimal effect on the environment. Technology since 432 BC has changed greatly, creating as many problems as opportunities for the environment. One of the modern-day problems that has developed as a result of all the advancements in technology is air pollution. Pollution has caused significant damage to the Parthenon, from biological, electrochemical, and chemical perspectives.

Biological damage is affecting the Parthenon in many different ways. Bird droppings, fungi, and even plant roots are reacting with the marble of the structure, resulting in erosion. Erosion causes the marble of the Parthenon to become worn down and dirty. It is important that the Parthenon be cleaned regularly to prevent further damage.

The Parthenon is exposed to many forms of pollution, including smog and car exhaust.

Electrochemical damage is caused by slowly evaporating water. Due to the humidity in Greece, moisture stays in the air for a long time. This water is causing the surface of the Parthenon's marble exterior to turn into gypsum, or hydrated calcium sulphate. Gypsum can be difficult to notice on the Parthenon because it is usually yellow or even colorless. The result is that much of the marble of the Parthenon is wearing down.

ACID RAIN

Acid rain is causing chemical damage to the Parthenon in the form of corrosion. This is most obvious on the inward-facing portions of the columns, where black crusts have formed. These black crusts are due to pollution from Athens. Since these portions are inward-facing, they receive considerably less rain than the outer parts of the columns.

Sulfur dioxide uptake occurs in the presence of the pollution and any moisture. Over time, this becomes sulfuric acid, which eats away at the marble. Metal oxides, soot, and even dust can be serious threats.

Each of these threats has the ability to stick to the marble and make changes to its color. By changing the appearance, it is more difficult to see the beautiful decorations and craftsmanship, as well as cracks that might be forming.

Construction Careers

Ictinus may have been the main architect on the Parthenon, but there were many others involved in building the structure. Among them were construction workers, carpenters, metalworkers, **quarry** workers, and **stonemasons**. The Parthenon took 15 years to build, and each of these people brought a specialty to the project that was very important.

Sculptors

Sculptors are artistic people who mold objects from a variety of materials, including marble and bronze. They decide on the materials that they would like to use and then make a sketch of the finished project they hope to create. After completing the rough sketch, they take the materials and begin working on them with a variety of tools. In ancient Greece, the tools were basic, such as a hammer that could strike a fine edge. With the advances in technology, sculptors have more options, but the principles and the art remain the same. Sculpting has become more organized. It is taught in various places, including university art classes, and there are many groups dedicated to it throughout the world.

Carpenters

Carpenters played an important role in the construction of the Parthenon. Each of the drums of the columns was joined by a wooden fastener. After a notch had been cut into the center of the drum, a carpenter would place a plug inside. Then, using an auger, or hand drill, the carpenter would make a hole in the plug. A circular, wooden pin was placed upright inside the hole. This pin would hold the drum in place when it was stacked as part of a column. Carpenters are important to construction today. They perform many different woodworking tasks. Some carpenters build the frames for buildings, such as houses. Other carpenters make furniture. Carpentry is often done outdoors, especially on buildings. Most carpenters learn the trade by working with others who are skilled at the craft.

Quarry Workers

Quarry workers used mallets and chisels to take stone from Mount Pentelicus. First, they cut grooves into the marble. Then, they hammered wooden wedges into the grooves and soaked them with water. As the grooves expanded, they would crack the marble. Using crowbars, the quarry workers pried the marble from the mountainside.

Web Link:
To find out more about a career in the skilled trades, visit www.bls.gov/oco/cg/cgs003.htm

Notable Structures

The Parthenon is considered by many to be one of the most important and unique structures ever built. Its innovative design and historical significance have influenced the building of many structures around the world.

Federal Hall

Built: 1842

Location: New York City, New York

Design: Ithiel Town, Alexander Jackson Davis, John Frazee

Description: Federal Hall uses Doric columns similar to those of the Parthenon. The building was the first Customs House in the United States. Today, it is a National Historic Site that is used as a museum.

The British Museum

Built: 1847

Location: London, England

Design: Robert Smirke

Description: The British Museum is an art and historical museum. The Elgin Marbles, originally taken from the Parthenon, are on display at the museum, which was built using stone and includes a copper-domed reading room.

The use of Doric columns and **Greek Revival Architecture** has been used to construct many structures, from churches to museums and statues.

The Parthenon

Built: 1897

Location: Nashville, Tennessee, United States

Design: William C. Smith

Description: Nashville's Parthenon is, in many ways, a tribute to the original. The building and its 42-foot (13-m) statue of Athena are full-scale replicas of the actual Parthenon. It was originally built for Tennessee's Centennial Exposition in 1897 and is currently an art museum.

Shrine of Remembrance

Built: 1934

Location: Melbourne, Australia

Design: Peter Hudson and James Wardrop

Description: The Shrine of Remembrance was built as a tribute to the men and women who served during wartime. Hudson and Wardrop won a competition to determine which design would be used for the Shrine of Remembrance. It is considered a Doric architectural design.

Structures Through History

Structures are found in every country of the world. Some are well-known because of their historical significance. Others are known for their innovative architectural design or their

Structure: Empire State Building
Location: New York City, United States
Year: 1931
Materials: stone with a steel frame

ARCTIC
OCEAN

NORTH
AMERICA

ATLANTIC
OCEAN

PACIFIC
OCEAN

SOUTH
AMERICA

Structure: Sears Tower
Location: Chicago, United States
Year: 1974
Materials: steel frame

621 Miles

0   1,000 Kilometers

impressive size, while still others for the materials used. This map outlines a few of the world's most important structures and illustrates the materials used.

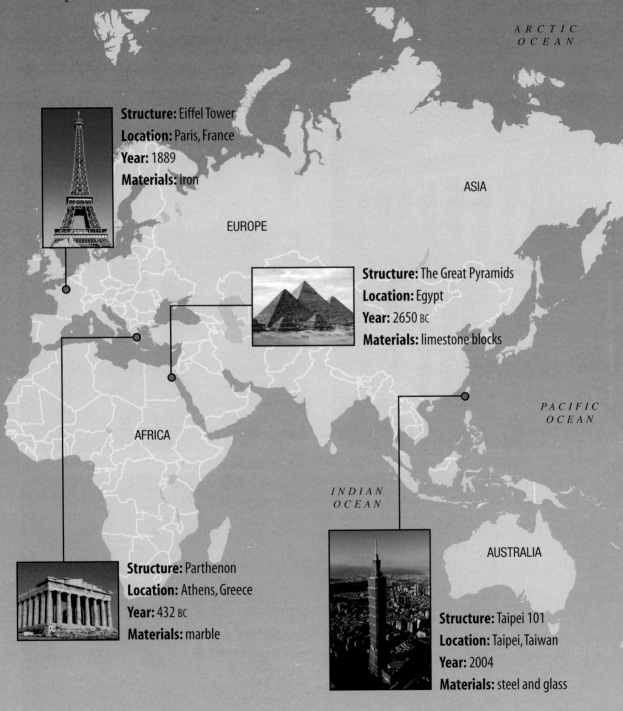

Structure: Eiffel Tower
Location: Paris, France
Year: 1889
Materials: iron

ARCTIC
OCEAN

ASIA

EUROPE

Structure: The Great Pyramids
Location: Egypt
Year: 2650 BC
Materials: limestone blocks

PACIFIC
OCEAN

AFRICA

INDIAN
OCEAN

AUSTRALIA

Structure: Parthenon
Location: Athens, Greece
Year: 432 BC
Materials: marble

Structure: Taipei 101
Location: Taipei, Taiwan
Year: 2004
Materials: steel and glass

Quiz

Q What are three main forms of environmental damage to the Parthenon?

A The three main forms of environmental damage are biological, electrochemical, and chemical.

Q What building ratio was used throughout the Parthenon?

A The 4:9 ratio (length:width) was used on the Parthenon.

Q Why were no straight lines used on the Parthenon?

A There are no straight lines on the Parthenon because vertical straight lines are seen as slightly slanted to the unaided eye.

Q How many tons of marble were used to build the Parthenon?

A More than 20,000 tons (18,000 tonnes) of marble were used.

Make A Golden Rectangle

Ictinus had a deep appreciation for math and science. He was one of the first people to use ratios in developing architectural designs. One of the ratios connected with the Parthenon is the Golden Rectangle. The Golden Rectangle is a ratio that is always 1:1.6. No matter how many times the point where two sides connect is moved, the ratio remains the same. Try this activity to explore the concept of the Golden Rectangle.

Materials
- a sheet of paper
- ruler
- pencil
- scissors

Instructions

1. Draw a rectangle on the sheet of paper, with the width being 6.5 inches (16.5 centimeters) and the length being 10.5 inches (27 cm).

2. Divide the length by the width. Your answer should be 1.6.

3. Use the pencil to draw a square inside the rectangle. The outer edge of the rectangle should make up one side of the square. Each side of the square should be 6.5 inches (16.5 cm), equal to the width of the rectangle.

4. Using the scissors, cut the square out of the page.

5. With the ruler, take the measurements of the remaining rectangle, and convert any fractions into decimals. To convert fractions into decimals, divide the top number by the bottom number.

6. Divide the length by the width. The result will once again be 1.6, as it was with the original example.

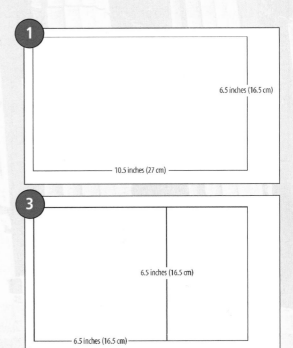

1

6.5 inches (16.5 cm)

10.5 inches (27 cm)

3

6.5 inches (16.5 cm)

6.5 inches (16.5 cm)

Further Research

You can find more information on the Parthenon and other structures at your local library or on the Internet.

Websites

For more information about the Parthenon, visit www.parthenontemple.com

To find out more about restoration work being done to the Acropolis, surf to http://ysma.culture.gr/english/index.html

Learn more about acid rain at www.epa.gov/acidrain

Glossary

acid rain: the result of a chemical transformation which occurs after sulfur dioxide and nitrogen oxides are emitted into the air and absorbed by water droplets in the clouds

Acropolis: the fortified part of a Greek city

architect: a person who designs buildings

Christian: a person who believes in and follows the teachings of Jesus Christ

contractor: a person or company hired to do work for another person or company

Corinthian: a style of column with a top that has leaves instead of the fine edges seen in other columns

cultures: groups of people that come from different places

diameter: the length of a line that passes through the center of a circle from one side to the other

element: a substance made of atoms

Greek Revival Architecture: a period in architectural history, occurring in the early nineteenth century, in which building styles from Ancient Greece were used

Ionic: a style of columns that is curved to make the column visually appealing

mosque: a Muslim place of worship

optical illusion: something that appears to be different from what it actually is

quarry: a place where stone is dug out for use in a building or sculpture

sculptor: a person who makes statues and other figures out of rock and other materials

stonemasons: people who prepare stones for a building

stylobate: a horizontal column of rock that supports a vertical column

treasury: a place for storing money and other valuable items

Index